Ragnar Lothbrok
A Legendary Viking Warrior, His Family, and His Legacy

DUSTIN YARC

The following book is reproduced below with the goal of providing information that is as accurate and as reliable as possible. Regardless, purchasing this book can be seen as consent to the fact that both the publisher and the author of this book are in no way experts on the topics discussed within, and that any recommendations or suggestions made herein are for entertainment purposes only. Professionals should be consulted as needed before undertaking any of the action endorsed herein.

This declaration is deemed fair and valid by both the American Bar Association and the Committee of Publishers Association and is legally binding throughout the United States.

Furthermore, the transmission, duplication or reproduction of any of the following work, including precise information, will be considered an illegal act, irrespective whether it is done electronically or in print. The legality extends to creating a secondary or tertiary copy of the work or a recorded copy and is only allowed with express written consent of the Publisher. All additional rights are reserved.

The information in the following pages is broadly considered to be a truthful and accurate account of facts, and as such any inattention, use or misuse of the information in question by the reader will render any resulting actions solely under their purview. There are no scenarios in which the publisher or the original author of this work can be in any fashion deemed liable for any hardship or damages that may befall them after undertaking information described herein.

Additionally, the information found on the following pages is intended for informational purposes only and should thus be considered, universal. As befitting its nature, the information presented is without assurance regarding its continued validity or interim quality. Trademarks that mentioned are done without written consent and can in no way be considered an endorsement from the trademark holder.

DEDICATION

For my wonderful readers.

CONTENTS

INTRODUCTION

Congratulations on purchasing your personal copy of *Ragnar Lothbrok*. Thank you for doing so.

The following chapters will discuss the Viking hero Ragnar Lothbrok. Specifically, this book addresses the real person who is believed to have lived in the 9th century. It is important to distinguish the historical figure of Ragnar Lothbrok from the fictional and dramatized character based off him, which appears in the 2013 television series *Vikings*.

In this book, you will discover the history of this 9th-century Danish king, whose name is still shrouded in many legends, even centuries after his death. Ragnar was famous for being a warlord and acquired his fortune by raiding the kingdoms of the West. He is said to have been merciless and even attacked people during prayer times at churches. You will learn about how he battled the Roman Emperor Charlemagne, and how he was eventually captured by Aella of Northumbria, an Anglo-Saxon king. You will also learn about Ragnar's three sons, who led an invasion on East Anglia to seek revenge for their father's death.

The final chapter will explore whether or not Ragnar was in fact a real person. We will cover facts as well as myths about Ragnar. You get to decide for yourself if you think this man really existed or not.

There are plenty of books on this subject on the market, thanks again for choosing this one! Every effort was made to ensure it is full of as much useful information as possible. Please enjoy!

1 A BRIEF VIKING HISTORY

To GET A feeling for the time and place that Ragnar Lothbrok existed in, it's worth taking a look at what the world was like during his time, and what it meant to be a Viking.

The homeland for the Vikings was Scandinavia which includes Denmark, Sweden, and modern Norway. The Vikings would travel vast distances, usually by river or sea. They would voyage north to Lapland, south to Iraq and North Africa, west to North America, and east to Russia. We learn about them through writings of people that encountered them in Asia and Europe, treaties, proverbs, sagas, poetry, and archaeology. They were very skilled boat-builders and craftsmen. They were also traders and very adventurous explorers.

The Viking Age lasted approximately from 800 to 1150 A.D., even though Scandinavian mercenaries, merchants, and adventurers were active after and before this time. The expansion during this period was due to trade, settlement, exploration, and warfare.

About 200,000 people moved away from Scandinavia to live in other places like Sicily, France (they were known as the Normans here), the islands around Britain, Scotland, England, Ireland, Iceland, Greenland, and Newfoundland (which is part of modern-day Canada). They traded with Muslims and fought for the Byzantine emperors of Constantinople (which is now called Istanbul). The legacy of the Vikings had ended by the end of the 11th century.

Historians have always disagreed about where the word Viking arose. The word is believed by some to mean "pirate raider", but also appears to derive from the Old Norse words of either "vik" (meaning an inlet) or "vkija" (meaning to move swiftly). These words both capture the general idea of who they are. They were fast moving sailors that used water as their highway. It took them around Europe's coasts and across the north part of the Atlantic. They traveled up the rivers to settle, raid, or trade. The Vikings often referred to the sea as "the whale road." Writers have called them heathens, sea wolves, sea rovers, the vast army, Northmen, Norsemen, and Danes.

Many Vikings chose to stay in the places they explored, and so they settled and prospered and became part of the people who make up the nation of Britain.

Much of our language today is derived from ancient Norse words, unbeknownst to most people. We named the days of the week after Norse gods. We have also adopted many of their words into our language such as scrawny, spud, lump, much, fog, down, bread, die, law, and egg.

Vikings are usually portrayed as warriors whose achievements included nothing but raiding and plundering.

In 793 A.D., terror rained down on Northumbria's Coast as Viking raiders attacked the monastery of St. Cuthbert on Lindisfarne. The monks were terrified and watched helplessly as invaders left with priceless treasures and captives. This was the first Viking raid in recorded history.

Vikings were known as Scandinavian pirates that preyed on communities along the coast of north-western Europe for more than two hundred years and made a reputation for themselves as savage and heartless warriors.

Their image was made ever more fearsome by the accounts of their victims that recorded the details of their attacks. Alcuin of York dramatically wrote about the raid on Lindisfarne as follows: "the church was spattered with the blood of the priests of God, despoiled of all its ornaments…given as a prey to pagan peoples." Christian chroniclers and writers never lost an opportunity to demonize the so-called pagan Vikings.

Historically, Vikings did carry out violent and destructive attacks. They did small raids against churches to large scale battles that involved countless warriors. They formed a sophisticated and complex culture. They were not just pirates. They traded with cultures that were from the Caspian Sea and Russia. They were explorers and sent ships across the Atlantic to the coast of North America five hundred years before Columbus ever thought about it. They were artists that created works of great beauty. They were poets that composed sagas and verses that told of their powers.

The Vikings came from what we now know as Sweden, Norway, and Denmark. This was hundreds of years before they were unified countries. Their land was very rural and not many towns existed at the time. They earned miserable, paltry wages by farming or fishing. With the advances that came along in the eight and nine hundreds, when boats becoming powered by sails instead of oars meant their ships could move faster in the water. Sails were added to their vessels, which were made with overlapping planks to make longships. These were shallow drafted and swift boats that could easily travel around inland and coastal waters and could land on the beach.

Why Viking men decided to follow their local chief in longships across the North Sea is not clear. It might have been from becoming overpopulated, as lands became divided so much that families could no longer make a living. It might have been a politically unstable place, as regional chiefs started to fight for dominance. It could also have been stories that were brought in by other merchants of riches that could be found in the settlements that were located further west. It was more than likely the combination of all of these. Whatever the reason, the Vikings set out and attacked Lindisfarne in 793, Scotland in 794, Ireland in 795, and France in 799.

These first victims did not originally call these attackers Vikings. The term Viking wasn't popular until the 11th century. They were called Normanni or Northmen, pagani or pagans, or Dani or Danes. This did not necessarily imply that the Vikings were only people that lived in Denmark.

The raids started out small just a few boats full of men that came home when they had collected sufficient plunder or if they encountered too much resistance. In the 850's they started staying through the winter along the Seine in France, in Ireland, and in southern England to establish places from where they began to control the inland areas.

The raids reached their peak after the 850s. They established fortified ports in Ireland that included Dublin. From here they controlled most of the eastern section of the island. They grew stronger in France since the kingdom there had been fractured politically. In 885 an army of Vikings surrounded and just about captured Paris.

They established Earls in Orkney in Scotland and invaded the Hebrides and Shetlands. A "micel here" or Great Army arrived in England in 865. The group was led by brothers Ivar the Boneless and Halfdan, sons of Ragnar Lothbrok. They took over England's kingdoms one at a time. The first one they overtook was Northumbria. They gained the capital of York in 866. The next was East Anglia and then Mercia. Wessex being ruled by Alfred was the only one that remained. Alfred being a religious bookworm became king after his three older brothers had either died or gotten sick doing battle during other Viking raids.

In January 878, Guthrum led the Great Army across the frontier and surprised Alfred at his estate at Chippenham. Alfred managed to escape, but he spent months sulking in the marshes at Athelney. England's independence looked like it might be at its end. But Alfred managed to gather an army and went on to defeat the Great Army at Edington. He then forced Guthrum to get baptized and become a Christian. Alfred was the only native ruler to gain the nickname of Great since he saved England from the Vikings.

England remained divided for 80 years. The Southwest and South were controlled by Wessex and its kings. The Vikings controlled the Midlands and North. Kings of Vikings ruled until Erik Bloodaxe was thrown out and killed in 954. Danish customs stayed there, and Scandinavian DNA is still found in that region that was known as Danelaw for centuries.

By the middle of the 11th-century, kingdoms started to appear in Sweden, Norway, and Denmark. The raids were beginning to die down. In the early 11th century, royal expeditions managed to conquer England again and placed Danish kings there. These included Canute, he ruled in Norway, Denmark, and England. Folk tales at the time said that he even had the power to command the ocean's tides. Vikings stayed in control of the majority of Scotland, most notably Orkney near Dublin. Normandy, France is where King Charles the Simple granted some land to the Norwegian, Rollo, who is an ancestor of William the Conqueror. They had control over a large section of Russia and Ukraine where Vikings had pushed through in the eight hundred's and made states near Kiev and Novgorod.

2 RAGNAR'S WIVES

A LL OF THE above sets a foundation from which we can view the history and myths surrounding the figure known as Ragnar Lothbrok.
Ragnar had three different wives: Lagertha who was a shieldmaiden, Thora Town-hart, and Aslaug known as the warrior queen. Thora Town-hart was a noblewoman and was the daughter of Earl Herrauor of Gotaland. Some accounts say that Ragnar also had a fourth wife, but not enough details are known to be discussed here. Ragnar's wives bore him an abundance of sons. The ones that are the most famous are Ivar the Boneless, Halfdan, Hvitserk, Ubba, Bjorn Ironside, Harald, Rognvald, Hastein, Agnar, Eric, Fridleiv, Vunvat Ragnarsen, and Radbard Ragnarsen are just some of the names that have been recorded as being his sons. Ragnar also had a couple of daughters by Lagertha. He had some daughters with the other wives, but there isn't any accurate information telling their names. The only two names that have appeared in some stories that may be his daughters are Alof Ragnarsdottir and Ragnhild Ragnarsdottir.

LAGERTHA

Lagertha was a robust and powerful woman who lived during the age of the Vikings. Lagertha was a real shield maiden that lived in Norway. She was the wife of Ragnar Lothbrok before they separated.

Lagertha fought with Ragnar in a battle against Fro, who was king of Sweden. This battle avenged the death of Ragnar's grandfather King Siward. Fro had invaded Norway, and he killed the former king. Fro publicly humiliated the women of the dead king's family by putting them in a brothel.

Naturally, Ragnar was furious upon hearing this news, and he gathered

5

his army and pursued this new enemy. When he arrived, Ragnar collected the abused women from Fro. They readied them for battle by putting them in men's clothing and gave them all swords and shields. They used their anger to avenge their family and themselves from the abuse they received from Fro. Ragnar, with the help of his female warriors, received vengeance for his grandfather Siward. Much of the success of this battle can be awarded to Lagertha. She was truly a hero of her day.

Lagertha, even though she was a woman, had the same courage as the men did and fought on the front lines along the bravest Vikings. Everyone was in awe of her sword skills. The only thing that gave her secret of not being a man away was her hair hanging down her back.

This small woman surprised everyone with her courage, and Ragnar took to her instantly. Lagertha had a large hound and huge bear that guarded her home, which she instructed to attack Ragnar when he originally went to see Lagertha one day. Ragnar had come prepared, and he killed the bear by stabbing it with a spear. He then wrapped his arms around the hound and choked it. Lagertha was beyond impressed with his strength and accepted his marriage proposal. Ragnar and Lagertha had three children. A son Fridleif, and two daughters whose names went unrecorded.

Ragnar never got over the fact that Lagertha told her animals to attack him and he eventually divorced her. She went back to her homeland and remarried. When Ragnar got home to Denmark, he was facing another civil war. Even though they had separated, Lagertha still wanted to help Ragnar, so she gave him 120 ships. She still loved Ragnar and offered her help to him. She would save Ragnar and his son Siward who was wounded in a counter-attack.

THORA TOWN-HART

Herraudr was a legendary Earl of Gotaland, and he had a daughter named Thora Twon-Hart.

She married Ragnar Lothbrok and is the reason he was nicknamed Lothbrok, more information about this a bit later. She is his second wife. It is not known how many women Ragnar had waiting in the wings, but he was often referred to as a lady's man.

Legend has it that Thora received a small lindworm from her father. As it grew, it began to circle her private chambers. A Lindworm is a two-legged, wingless dragon who has poisonous venom like a Komodo dragon.

Thora's father promised her to the person who was able to slay the serpent. It was at this time when Ragnar wore his famous hairy breeches. This was what gave him the nickname Lothbrok, which loosely translates as hairy breeches.

The famous stories tell about Ragnar going to Vastergotland or West

Gothland and putting on shaggy clothes that had been coated with tar and sand. With a spear in hand he approached Thora's serpent, which spat poison at him. Ragnar's clothing protected him from the venom, and he was able to get close enough to the serpent to stick a spear into its heart. He then proceeded to cut off its head and then married Thora.

Ragnar and Thora had two sons, Agnar and Eirikr. Both sons perished while battling Eysteinn Beli who was king of Sweden at the time.

Before this took place, Thora died from an illness. This was when Ragnar married his third wife, Aslaug. She was the daughter of Brynhildr and Sigurd.

ASLAUG

As stated above, The shieldmaiden Aslaug was the daughter of Brynhildr and Sigurd parents. It is said that she was raised by a foster parent named Heimer. When both Byrnhildr and Sigurd had died, Heimer was worried about Aslaug's safety. He created a harp that was large enough to hold the girl. Heimer then went from town to town as a poor harp player, with Aslaug inside the instrument.

When they arrived in Spangereid in Norway, they stayed overnight with some peasants Grima and Ake. Ake thought that the harp was full of valuables and relayed this to his wife. Grima talked Ake into murdering Heimer while he slept. When they broke open the harp, they found Aslaug. They raised her as their own and changed her name to Kraka or Crow. They tried to hide her beauty by rubbing her with tar and making her wear a long hood.

One day while she was taking a bath, she was seen by Ragnar's men. They were so taken by her beauty that they burned the bread they were supposed to be baking. When Ragnar asked them about why they let the bread burn, and they told him about seeing the girl. Ragnar sent for her. He wanted to test her cleverness, so he told her to come not dressed or undressed, not fasting or eating, and not alone or with a company. She showed up wearing a net, taking a bite out of an onion and with a dog by her side. Ragnar was so impressed by her cleverness that he thought she would be a wise companion. He proposed marriage then, but she refused him until he had finished the mission in Norway. Aslaug refused to have sex with Ragnar until after they were married. Ragnar insisted on having sex with her immediately after they were married. She advised him to wait, but he refused and thus their first born son Ivar was born very weak and got the nickname of Boneless. Aslaug also had some preternatural wisdom. She made the shirt that protected Ragnar for a while when he was thrown into a pit of snakes, after having foreseen the event.

They had five sons: Sigurd Snake-in-the-eye, Bjorn Ironside, Ubba,

Hvitserk, and Ivar the Boneless.

3 RAGNAR'S SONS

RAGNAR HAD THREE wives, and each wife gave him sons and daughters. The daughter's names are unknown but following is a list of his wives, and the sons each gave him:

- Lagertha gave him Fridleif.

- Thora gave him two sons: Eric and Agnar.

- Aslaug gave him five sons: Ivar the Boneless, Bjorn Ironside, Hvitserk/Halfdan Ragnarsson, Ubba, and Sigurd Snake-in-the-Eye.

ERIC AND AGNAR

When Ragnar's sons grew up, they wanted to prove themselves to be equal to their father. They conquer Oland and all the small islands, Gotland, Reidgotaland, and Zealand. Ivar was the oldest and also the most clever. He was their leader and named himself as such at Lejre.

Ragnar didn't want to be overshadowed by his sons, so he appointed Eysteinn Beli as king of Sweden and ordered him to protect it from them. When Ragnar was pillaging through the Baltic region, Agnar and Eric went into Lake Malaren. They sent a messenger to ask Eysteinn to meet with them. They demanded Eysteinn be their servant and wanted his daughter Borghild to be Eric's wife. Eysteinn talked with his chieftains and they made a decision to attack Agnar and Eric. Agnar was killed, and Eric was captured after a long battle.

Eysteinn wanted peace and finally, offered Borghild to Eric and as much land as Eric wanted. Eric declined and asked to be put on spear points over his slain brother so that he would die. They gave him his wish.

Aslaug and her sons heard about the news in Zealand, and wanted to avenge their dead brothers. Aslaug changed her name to Randalin and took 1500 warriors across the land at the same time that her sons leave on ships. They fought a very long battle but finally killed Eysteinn. Agnar and Eric were avenged.

IVAR THE BONELESS

Ivar the Boneless was a great leader of Vikings and a legendary commander of the Great Heathen Army. He was the eldest son of Aslaug and Ragnar. He had four younger brothers. Even though he was known as a fierce warrior, he has also been described as being the wisest of all of Ragnar's children.

Ivar was also known as a berserker. These were warriors who would go into a trance of fury when fighting and this is where the English word berserk is derived from.

There are several stories about the origin of Ivar's nickname of "the boneless."

Some think that he was impotent. This is a bit far-fetched, however Ivar was never married and didn't have any children, so this could very well be the reason.

Another story is that Ivar was such a skilled warrior and was very flexible much like a snake and that was why he was called boneless. A poem that was written in the 1300's described Ivar as not having any bones whatsoever.

Another theory about his nickname was a result of a curse that was foreseen by his mother, Aslaug. Aslaug had the power of foresight.

Aslaug warned Ragnar not to consummate their marriage for three days. She said it would not please the gods and the child would be cursed. Ragnar, of course, ignored the warning and when Ivar was born, his legs were not made of bones, but instead they were made of a cartilage-like material.

When it came time to avenge his father's death, Ivar decided he didn't want to take part in it, since he knew that was the way Ragnar was destined to die. He went to King Aella and made peace with him and asked the king for some land. Just enough land that an ox hide would be able to cover it. King Aella thought Ivar was very foolish and granted this request. Ivar cut the hide in a way that by the time he was through, all Ivar's men were able to build a fort on the land that it encircled. It is said this land is York. Other accounts say that York was already built and Ivar just took it from the English.

Ivar wasn't just wise but was also a very generous leader. This was how he was able to recruit so many local English warriors for his forces and thus to weaken King Aella's forces with time.

One theory surrounding Ivar's death is that he died from a sudden disease in 873. It was suggested later in the 19th century that Ivar may have died from brittle bone disease. This could very well have been the reasoning behind him being called boneless.

BJORN IRONSIDE

Bjorn was a king of Sweden that lived in the 9th century. The protohistoric Swedish dynasty called the Munso Dynasty was founded by Bjorn.

Bjorn was a fearless warrior and also a fierce ruler just like his father. Bjorn pillaged and raided a wide variety of places including the coasts of North Africa, Sicily, cities in the Mediterranean Sea, Wales, England, Italy, Spain, and France. Bjorn was given the name Ironside after he came through a particularly gruesome battle unscathed.

Hastein is a man thought to be either a son of Ragnar or someone that Ragnar has assigned to be Bjorn's mentor. Bjorn and Hastein raided France and sailed into the Mediterranean. When they had finished raiding the coasts of Spain, they returned to France to pillage it again before they moved to the city of Pisa, Italy. They fought all the way up to the gates of Luna, which they thought was Rome. Conquering Luna is one of Bjorn's most significant battles. He captured the city using intelligence and great strategy, as opposed to sheer power. This is the greatest aspect that turned him into one of the most famous Vikings in history.

Bjorn was having problems getting through Luna's walls. Bjorn had to think about a clever way to get inside the city. He had his men go to the bishop and tell him that Bjorn had died, and that he had converted before he died and requested to be interred in the sacred ground. The bishop allowed the body to be brought inside by a group of guards that had swords under their robes. Upon entering the church, Bjorn jumped out of the box and surprised everyone. He fought all the way to the gates of the city. He opened the gates and gave his army entry into Luna and thus captured the city.

After they had conquered Luna, Bjorn and his fleet raided the coasts of North Africa and Sicily. As they were going back home, they met the forces of Al-Andalus at the Straits of Gibraltar. This was unfortunate for Bjorn because they were hit with a weapon called Greek fire. This is a weapon that will continue to burn even in water. This Greek fire took out 40 ships of Bjorn's fleet.

After Ragnar's death, all of his sons divided up the kingdom, and this is how Bjorn became the ruler of Uppsala and Sweden. Bjorn had two sons,

Refil and Erik Bjornsson. Erik became King of Sweden when Bjorn died.

Bjorn Ironside was the founder of the House of Munso in Sweden. This is also known as the Old Dynasty and ruled Sweden for several generations until they were thrown out after a long civil war through the 10th century. This dynasty eventually became the house of Denmark with time. The name Munso comes from an island where there is a hill which is claimed to be Bjorn's gravesite.

SIGURD SNAKE-IN-THE-EYE

Sigurd Snake-in-the-Eye was a son of Ragnar who was another great Viking King. The main difference between him and his brothers is that he had a defect with his left eye's pupil, which supposedly caused it to look like an ouroboros, or the image of a snake eating its own tail. Aslaugh, his mother, foretold this.

Sigurd and his father were very close. He went with his father on many dangerous expeditions; this led him through Russia all the way to Hellespont. In his later life, he went on a layover in Scottish Islands and Scotland, like most wise men did.

King Aella of Northumbria killed Sigurd's father Ragnar when he captured Ragnar and threw him in a pit of snakes. While Ragnar was in much pain and suffering, he is said to have yelled: "How the young pigs would squeal if they knew what the old boar suffers!" He was referring to the revenge that his sons would have on King Aella when they found out about his death.

King Aella was foolish and sent word to his sons. When Ragnar's sons heard about their father's death, Sigurd was so angered that he cut himself all the way through to his bone with a knife he was holding. Bjorn was holding his spear so tightly that there were imprints left behind in the wood from his fingers.

All of the men agreed that they would have their revenge for his death. This is a Viking tradition that carried through many generations. They marched across the North Sea with the Great Heathen Army in 866. The Great Heathen Army attacked York, found King Aella and seized him. He was then sentenced to be killed by way of Rista Blodam, meaning the Blood Eagle. This is a brutal and ritualistic form of Viking execution where the ribs are severed from the spine, and the lungs are then pulled through the opening in the back to create the appearance of a pair of wings.

Upon returning to Denmark, Sigurd and his brothers divided their father's kingdom between them. Sigurd ruled over Agder, Fjord, Oslo, Halland, Skane, Zealand and a large part of the uplands in Norwegia. Sigurd took King Aella's daughter Heluna to be his wife. The two had two children, Harde-Knud and Aslaug. Aslaug was named after her grandmother. Harde would become King of Sweden and Denmark.

Sigurd and his brothers kept raiding in several countries like Lombardy, France, Wales, and England. They had thought about going to Rome and trying to conquer it. They had plenty of famous battles that spread throughout various Norse countries. They are also known for carrying a banner with a raven on it into battle. Their sisters made the banner in just one afternoon. The raven would flap its wings if they were going to win their battle. The raven would stay still if it was destined for them to lose.

While in battled Emperor Arnulf in 891 in Leuven, Sigurd Snake-in-the-Eye died as well as 100,000 Norwegians and Danes. Helgi Hvassi, known as the Sharp, managed to escape with their standard, his shield, and weapon. He returned to Denmark and told Sigurd's mother's of his fate.

Aslaug said:

"Sad sit the corpse-stalkers,
Slaverers after cadavers:
The slain-craver, raven
What a shame! – forsaken
By namesake of Sigurd;
In vain now they're waiting.
Too soon from life Lord Odin
Let such a hero go."

Harthacanute inherited his father's throne to become the King of Halland, Zealand, and Scania. The land of Viken was lost. Harthecanute fathered Gorm the Old, who was also a King of Denmark.

Aslaug, Sigaurd's daughter, was married to Helgi the Sharp. She gave birth to a son. They named him Sigurd Hart. Years later, Sigurd Hart would be killed by Haki, the berserker, and he would take Sigurd's children, Gutorm and Ragnhild. Before he had the chance to marry Ragnhild, 15-years-old, she was taken again by Halfdan the Black. Harald Fairhar, was the first King of Norway, his parents were Ragnhild and Halfdan.

HALFDAN RAGNARSSON

Halfdan Ragnarsson was a commander of the Great Heathen Army and a Viking leader that invaded several kingdoms of England from 865. He was one of Ragnar's sons born of Aslaug. He became the first King of Northumbria and claimed the Kingdom of Dublin. He was killed in 877 during the Battle of Strangford Lough where he was trying to press his claim over Ireland.

While Ivar was in Ireland, this left Halfdan to be the main commander of the Great Heathen Army. In 870 Halfdan led the army to invade Wessex. The army battled the Saxons nine times. Since they could not defeat the West Saxons, Halfdan decided to accept a truce with Alfred, the newly crowned King of Wessex.

The Army went back to London. They remained there throughout the winter of 871 – 872. The coins that were minted during this time have Halfdan's name on them and identify him as the army's leader.

Following the victory of Mercia in 874, the army split with half of it under Guthrum's leadership and the other half under Halfdan. Halfdan headed north to fight the Britons and Picts of Strathclyde. Eystein, King of Dublin, was killed in 875 deceitfully by "Albann" a person who has been said to be Halfdan. Halfdan had been trying to win back his brother's kingdom because Ivar had ruled the city before he died in 873. Whether or not he got it doesn't matter since Halfdan did not stay in Ireland. In 876 he returned to Northumbria and stayed in a city that, for the most part, stayed compatible with the kingdom of Deira. The north part of Northumbria remained under the Anglo-Saxon rule. Some sources give Halfdan the title of King of Jorvik or York starting in 876.

It looks like Halfdan's rule over Dublin wasn't as secure as he thought it was. He was dethroned while in York. When he went back to Ireland in 877, he tried to recapture it but was stopped by an army of Fair Heathens. This term refers to the Viking population that had been in Ireland for a long time instead of the Dark Heathens which Halfdan was considered to be one of. These armies faced each other at the Battle of Strangford Lough, where he, unfortunately, was killed. The men of Halfdan's group that survived returned to Northumbria by way of Scotland. They fought a battle on their way where Constantine I, the King of the Picts was slain. It would seem that the Vikings of Northumbria were just content to stay kingless until about 883 when Guthfrith was named king.

HVITSERK

Hvitserk, the White Shirt, was a son of the 9th-century legend Ragnar Lothbrok and Aslaug. He is never mentioned in any of the places that mention Halfdan. Some scholars have speculated that Hvitserk and Halfdan are actually the same person.

After he had helped his brothers avenge their father's death, he went to Gardarike. He also pillaged with the Rus. He was faced with a large opposition and new he couldn't win. When they asked him how he wanted to die, he told them we wanted to be burnt alive.

UBBA

Ubba or Ubbe was a Viking chieftain in the 800's and was a commander of the Great Heathen Army. This army was a combination of Viking warriors that invaded Northumbria and surrounding kingdoms in 865.

Many English sources describe the men as heathens and Danes, but there is no firm evidence that suggests that the forces started in Frisia. Once source describes Ubba as the dux (or leader) of the Frisians. In the year of 865, the Great Heathen Army that was led by Ivar stayed the winter in East Anglia before they invaded and destroyed Northumbria. After the Mericans gave them what they wanted in 869, the Vikings overtook the East Angles. Their king, Edmund was killed. Edmund was later called a saint. Most sources don't associate Ubba with this campaign; some other sources do associate him with the king's martyrdom.

After the East Anglian kingdom had fallen, the leadership of the Great Heathen Army fell to Halfdan, Ivar's brother. The Vikings then warred with the West Saxons and destroyed Mercia. In 873 the Great Army split. Halfdan went north, and Guthrum went west. Guthrum launched an attack deep in Wessex, which might have been helped along by another Viking force in Devon. According to sources, this force was led by Ivar and Halfdan's brother Ubba.

Some ninth century sources show that Vikings ruined Frisia in 851 and another one states that a force of Frisians and Danes hit land on the Isle of Sheppey in 855. The same source says that in the tenth and eleventh centuries say that Ubba as dux of the Frisians.

One article calls the army micel here, while another uses the term Scaldingi and this means people from the River Scheldt. This shows that Ubba might just have been from Walcheren which is an island at the mouth of the Scheldt. Danish Vikings were known to have lived on this island twenty years earlier. Emperor Lothair I gave the island to Harald in 841. If Ubba's troops had been drawn out of the Frisian settlement that was started by Harald 20 years before, many of Ubba's men might just have been born in Frisia.

4 THE SIEGE OF PARIS

A FLEET CONTAINING 120 Viking ships with 5,000 or more men entered the Seine under Ragnar's command in March 845. Around the year 841, Charles the Bald gave Ragnar land in Turholt, Frisia. He lost this land and subsequently the king's favor. Ragnar and the Vikings raided Rouen as they went up the Seine. Charles assembled an army that he divided into two separate parts. He put one on each side of the river. He was trying to keep the Vikings away from the Abbey of Saint-Denis which is near Paris so they wouldn't destroy it. Ragnar did in fact attack and defeated the smaller army. Ragnar took 111 Frankish men as prisoners and hung them on a Seine island. They did this to honor Odin, a Norse god and to inflict terror into the remaining Franks.

The Vikings arrived on Easter Sunday, March 29 in Paris. They entered and plundered the city. A plague broke out during the siege. Since they had been exposed to Christianity, they did what one of the Christian prisoners suggested, and they first tried praying to the Norse gods, and then they fasted. The plague decreased. The Franks were not able to muster a large enough army together to defeat the Vikings, and decided to pay them off. The Vikings left after they were paid 7,000 livres of gold and silver by Charles. This is equal to about 5,670 pounds or 2,570 kilograms. Since Charles had taken back land from Ragnar, this payment might have been compensation for this loss. The invasion may have been an act of revenge. This is the first of thirteen payments of Danegeld to the Vikings by the Franks. Even though Ragnar agreed to leave Paris, he still pillaged many cities on the coast as they returned which included the Abbey of Saint Bertin.

Charles was criticized heavily for giving the huge ransom payment. He had more issues that he had to deal with as well, such as pressures from other countries and disputes with his brothers. Charles had trouble trusting his people to gather and lead an army to try to defeat Ragnar's large army. So he knew that paying them off would buy him some time and just possibly give him peace from other Viking raids.

During the same year, another Viking fleet attacked Hamburg. Hamburg had been raised to Archbishop status by Pope Gregory IV in 831 on the promise of Louis the Pious that he would take care of the Saxon lands and introduce the Scandinavians to Christianity. Louis the German, the East Frankish King, sent a mission that was led by Count Cobbo to Horik and demanded that he submit to the Frankish lordship and pay for the invasion. Horik finally agreed to his terms and asked for a peace treaty. He also promised to give back the captives and treasures from the raid. Horik wanted to secure the Saxon border since he was facing a conflict with King Olof of Sweden. Louis demanded the obedience of Horik. This was secured by Horik sending gifts to Louis and his promise of suspending his support of the Vikings.

Many Vikings died during the plague that befell them during the Paris siege. Ragnar returned home to King Horik. Ragnar attacked the Abbey of Saint-Germain-des-Pres which is located on the outskirts of Paris. Cobbo visited the Abbey later and said the plague was caused by the power of Saint Germain of Paris. Ragnar showed the silver and gold he had gotten and boasted about how easy the conquest had been. He collapsed crying while he was telling about the resistance he met by the deceased saint. Many of Ragnar's men died shortly after returning home. King Horik was so scared he ordered all the survivors to be executed and he released all of the Christian captives. This led to Horik inviting Archbishop Ansgar into his kingdom on friendly terms.

Vikings would come back time and time again during the 860's to get ransom or loot. As a turning point in France's history, the city walls held against the largest Viking attack in the Siege of Paris 885 - 886.

5 PLUNDERING THE BRITISH ISLES

THERE HAS BEEN a lot of debate about what caused the Viking expansion. One idea is that it was retaliation toward the Europeans for their invasion of Scandinavia. Charlemagne invaded Scandinavia trying to get the pagans converted to Christianity. If they refused, they were killed. It is not a mere coincidence that the early activity happened while Charlemagne was reigning. The invasion of Christianity in Scandinavia created major conflicts and caused a division in Norway for about one hundred years. Note that the target of the first raids was not France but the monasteries in and around England. This seems rather inconsistent with revenge but would be normal for religious warfare.

Another story is that the population of Scandinavia had outgrown their lands. There was not enough land for farming, and many families found that they were beginning to starve. Some say that this could have been true for western Norway because there were few parcels of land, but it was probably not the case in the rest of Scandinavia.

Another story says that the expansion was driven by the fact that the younger sons of families needed to go elsewhere to find fortune. The oldest sons always got the family's estate, and that left the younger ones nowhere to live when they were ready to marry and start a family of their own. Most of the Vikings emigrated because they wanted to own more land instead of just the need to have it.

It doesn't matter what caused the emigration. Research has shown that all of these were demonstrated during this period. It is not clear why these pressures would have caused the expansion to go overseas instead of trying to cultivate the forest of the interior region in the Scandinavian Peninsula. Raids might just have given them more profits and been easier than clearing the forest to make more farms and pastures since they did have a limited growing season.

One theory that goes against these shortcomings could be that the Scandinavians may have practiced selective procreation which leads to a shortage of females. Their main motive was to find wives. This doesn't explain why some of the Vikings chose to live in other countries instead of just bringing women back to Scandinavia.

It could be possible that they had seen a decline in the profits along with their old trade routes and this caused them to seek out some new ones that would bring them more profit. Trade with western Europe and the main part of Eurasia might have suffered once the Roman Empire lost all of its western countries in the four hundred's. Islam's expansion in the eight hundred's might have lessened their trade opportunities with Western Europe by detouring the resource on the Silk Road. Trade along the Mediterranean Sea was at a low point when the Vikings started their raids. The Vikings opened many trade routes throughout Arab and French lands. They took over the markets that used to be controlled by the Frisians after France had destroyed the Frisian fleet.

While King Beortric of Wessex was in reign, they had three ships land at Portland Bay in Dorset. The local steward thought the Vikings were just merchants and showed them where the royal estate was. Before he could warn the others, these Northmen killed both him and his men. The earliest planned raid happened on January 6, 793. It targeted the monastery at Lindisfarne that is located off the north-east coast in Northumbria. The Vikings killed the monks that lived there. They also chose the just throw them into the sea to either drown or be carried downstream to become slaves. The monks finally decided to leave Lindisfarne in 875 after they had endured eighty years of Viking raids. They took the Treasures of Saint Cuthbert with them.

A small fleet of Vikings, in 794, attacked a monastery in Jarrow. They ended up facing a stronger resistance than they thought they would. The leaders were slain. The warriors managed to escape just to find that their crew had been slain by some locals, and their ships beached on Tynemouth. This ended up being one of their last raids in England for almost forty years. The Vikings chose to focus on Scotland and Ireland during this time.

A group of uncoordinated Vikings joined to create one army and landed in East Anglia. This was the start of the Great Heathen Army. This army was led by Ivar the Boneless, Guthrum, Halfdan, and Bjorn Ironside. They went through the Midlands into Northumbria and managed to capture York. Some of the Vikings decided to settle there as farmers. Since the majority of the English kingdoms were in turmoil due to a civil war, they could not withstand the Viking forces. King Alfred managed to defeat this Great Heathen Army in Edington in 878. The Treaty of Wedmore was signed in 878. The Treaty of Alfred and Guthrum was signed in 886. These finalized the boundaries of English kingdoms and the Viking Danelaw territory. These provided the Vikings and the English to have peaceful relations with each other. Despite these treaties, the conflict did continue. Alfred did eventually drive the Vikings back and took York back.

All of the Vikings that arrived in England and Ireland did not come as raiders. Some of them arrived with livestock and families. Most often after one of the territories had been captured by the Vikings. The population within these areas started to merge with time, and many intermarriages with the Anglo-Saxon people became the norm. Many of the words in the English language came from the old Scandinavian language, and this shows the importance of the contact these two cultures created.

RAGNAR LOTHBROK

6 RAGNAR'S DEATH

THERE ARE A couple of different stories about Ragnar's death. One says he died from succumbing to the injuries he sustained during the raid on Paris. Others say he died of a deadly disease like diarrhea after he raided Paris. The diseases description and the details on how he died that were given in many different accounts all point to dysentery as the cause of death.

The other one is told in many different historical accounts. They all tell us that Ragnar met his death at the hands of his enemies. They are all the same story just told in a couple of different ways.

One version of this story says that on the way back from Paris, his ship washed ashore on a coast of Northumbria. He had attacked this kingdom several times and had made them pay a ransom. King Aella had wanted to get revenge on Ragnar for a very long time. He was able to capture Ragnar and throw him in the snake pit thus leaving him to a very painful death.

One legend says that just before he died, Ragnar sang a Norse hymn and informed King Aella that he would be avenged by his sons.

Another story states that King Aella of Northumbria finds out about the pillaging army and he gathers a large army to defeat Ragnar's army. Ragnar is wearing a silk jacket that Aslaug made, and nothing can go through it. When his army is defeated, he is taken as a prisoner and thrown into a pit of snakes. The snakes can't bite him through the jacket. King Aella had his men take his clothes off and then the snakes kill him. King Aella had Ragnar thrown to the snakes because Ragnar boasted about the serpent he killed spitting venom at him and its venom not harming him.

Even after Ragnar's death, his descendants continued to make an impact on the region. His legacy continued. Ragnar's descendants moved to

23

the west coast of France somewhere around two centuries after his death and turned the area into the Land of the Northmen or Normandy as we call it today.

7 REVENGE OF THE GREAT HEATHEN ARMY

IVAR THE BONELESS was the original leader of the Great Heathen Army that invaded what we now know as England.

Ivar was the son of Ragnar and Aslaug. He, his brothers, and his half-brothers, Bjorn Ironside, Halfdan Ragnarsson, Hvitserk, Sigurd Snake-in-the-Eye and Ubba had grown up and wanted to prove that they were equal to their father.

These brothers warred and raided far and wide. They conquered places like Oland and the surrounding islands, Gotland, Reidgotaland or Jutland, and Zealand.

Ivar was the leader because he was the most clever.

Most of the Viking raids were mostly hit and run before 865. In 865 they changed from just raids to invasions and had the intent to conquer the land. Pressure from the kings in the Nordic regions had forced them to seek out new places to start new lives. These Norsemen were looking for lands where they could settle with their families and have a farm.

One legend about Ragnar's sons says that the attention Ragnar's sons gave England was due to the death of their father. Ragnar was captured by King Aella during a raid and then thrown into a snake pit to die.

The year following Ragnar's death, Ivar built a substantial army and sought revenge for the father against King Aella.

Ivar started building this army when he asked King Aella to give him some land and he built the city of York. Throughout the years, Ivar gained favor with the Englishmen because he was a very generous leader. When he knew he had enough men, he sent for is brothers to attack Northumbria again.

In 865, this Great Heathen Army had been formed by unordered groups of Vikings that came from various countries including Denmark,

Norway, and Sweden. Their leaders were Ragnar's sons Ivar, Hafldan, Ubbe, and Bjorn. They also had the help of Dane Viking chieftain Guthrum.

All these men were aware of the war that had weakened the northern kingdom of England. These Norse warriors were known for being opportunistic.

These Vikings joined forces and came in and stayed the winter in East Anglia. To protect their land, the East Anglians made a peace treaty with the Great Heathen Army. They also wanted to see their enemies attacked. They permitted the Vikings to stay on their land and to gather their army there. They also provided horses for them. The Vikings used this as a beginning point of their invasion of Northumbria.

Toward the end of 866, the Great Heathen Army was ready to march into Northumbria. On November 21st they seized Jorvik or York. York had a huge defensive wall around it that the Roman Army had built. Kings Osberht and Aella joined their armies and tried to take York from the Vikings on March 21st 867. Just two day later on March 23, 867, they continued to retake York, but the battle ended with King Osberht getting killed and King Aella was captured alive.

The brothers thought that carving the blood eagle would be a good punishment for King Aella. This is done by laying the victim on their stomach, cutting down the spine, breaking the ribs, and pulling the lungs out to resemble wings. Then they just watched and waited for him to die. They subjected him to this as punishment for throwing their father into the snake pit a year earlier.

After they won the battle and gained control of the region once again, the Northumbrians paid the Vikings what they wanted and the Great Heathen Army appointed leaders. They appointed King Egbert as a tax collector and puppet leader for Northumbria.

They then went to the Kingdom of Mercia. In 867 they took control of Nottingham.

The king of Kent and Mercia, King Burgred asked for help from his brother-in-law King Aethelred I who was the king of Wessex the help defend against these Viking invaders.

King Aethelred and his brother Alfred who will later become Alfred the Great, led the West Saxon army from Mercia and Wessex and took hold of Nottingham without any clear results. The Mercians ended up paying the Vikings to leave.

The Great Heathen Army went back to Northumbria in the fall of 868 and stayed there through the winter. They stayed in York for the majority of 869. Many stayed hoping to start a new life there, but others sought lands of their own. This was the main reason they had come there in the first place. Their leaders had assured them that there was plenty of land available.

The Great Heathen Army went back to East Anglia and stayed through the winter of 869 – 870 at the Isle of Thetford. When they arrived, there was not a peace treaty with the East Anglians and the Viking army. These East Anglians were not caught by surprise. The Great Heathen Army wasn't as great this time as they had lost many of their numbers. They saw this as the perfect time to rebel against the Vikings. King Edmund fought against them, but it didn't do any good.

The king was captured, but he refused to renounce his Christianity. He said his faith was more important to him than his life. He was crucified and then shot with arrows until he died. After they had subdued the East Anglians, the Great Heathen Army decided to stay through the winter there and started preparing to attack other Anglo lands as soon as warmer weather allowed.

The Battle of Englefield took place on December 31st, 870 at Englefield which is near Reading. This is now the county of Berkshire. This was just one of many battles that took place after the invasion of Wessex by the Danish army. The Danes made camp at Reading during these battles.

Three days after arriving in Reading, the Danes led by two jarls rode toward Englefield. Aethelwulf had gathered forces and was waiting for them here. During this battle, a lot of the Danes were killed including Sidrac and the rest were forced back to Reading.

This victory for the Saxon did not last too long. Just four days later the big West Saxon army that was led by King Ethelred and Alfred the Great attacked the main camp at Reading and soon became extremely bloody. Both sides lost many people that day including Aethelwulf.

In 871 King Bagsecg came from Scandinavia and brought the Great Summer Army. He added them to the Great Heathen Army who had already had a lot of success in taking over most of England.

The Vikings then moved to London to stay through the winter in 872 before they moved back to Northumbria in 873. A rebellion formed against their puppet leader, so they returned so they could retake power. They set up home for the winter in Torksey located in Lindsey which is now a part of Lincolnshire in 872 – 873. The Mercians paid them for their peace. By the end of 873, they made their winter dwellings at Repton in Derbyshire.

After their stay through the winter in Repton, they pushed the Mercian king into exile and was able to take over Mercia. Ceowulf replaced this Mercian king.

They returned to Mercia and conquered it in 874. They stayed through the winter at Repton that's on the River Trent. The kingdom of Wessex was the only kingdom that had yet to be conquered by the Vikings. Toward the end of 875, the army started the second invasion of Wessex. Alfred the Great had experienced some problems, but the finally defeated them in the

Battle of Edington. They agreed to a treaty stating that the Vikings could keep control of most of the eastern and northern England.

The Vikings decided to split the army. Halfdan took one-half north back to Northumbria where he stayed through the winter on the River Tyne in 874 – 875. In 875 he decided to raid into Scotland. He battled the Britons and Picts of Strathclyde. He returned south below the border in 876. He divided out Northumbria among his men, who decided to plow the land and support their families this is part of the land that was later known as the Danelaw.

The other half of the army that was led by Guthrum, Anwend and Oscetel, would leave Repton in 874 and took up residence in Cambridge to stay at through the winter of 874 – 875. In the latter part of 875, they started moving toward Wareham. They invaded Wareham and build a fortification for their position. Alfred worked to make a treaty with them so that they would remove themselves from Wessex. They did decide to leave Wareham, but they didn't stay gone for long. They went onto raid different areas of Wessex, and, before long, were successful. In 878, Alfred fought back at the Battle of Edington, and won. This was followed by the Treaty of Wedmore. This caused England to be divided between the Vikings and the Anglo-Saxons. Guthrum was also baptized.

Later in 878, Guthrum's army moved to Cirencester, in Mercia. In 879, they traveled to East Anglia. Guthrum, Aethelstan as he was later known as, reigned as King there until his death in 890.

The army members that didn't travel to Guthrum start to settle in York and Northumbria. Some decided to settle in Mercia. The reason this is known is because of the Viking cemeteries located in Derbyshire, one in Repton, and the other in Heath Wood.

Excavations at a monastery in Repton during 1974 to 1988 found a D-shaped mound on located at the river bank; that had been worked into the church. Viking burials were performed at the east part of the church. A building that they tore down and turned into a part of their cemetery was uncovered and 249 people were found buried there. The long bones had been positioned to point towards the center of the grave. At the center of the grave stood a stone coffin, but the remains didn't survive. They studied the remains and found that around 80% belonged to men, aged between 15 and 45. Further investigation discovered they had no relation to the locals of Repton, but instead were probably Scandinavian. The remains of the females showed that they were similar to the locals which suggested Anglo-Saxon heritage. It's possible that these people might have suffered an epidemic during the winter of 873 – 874 which lead to the mass burial. In the nearby cemetery of Heath Wood, they found around sixty cremations instead of burials. Findings of cremations in the British Isles were very rare, and this one points to it being the war cemetery of the Great Heathen

Army.

    Ivar and Olaf the White ruled Dublin. They sieged Dumbarton Rock which was also known as Clyde Rock in Scotland. Even though they resisted for several months, they had to surrender because the Vikings cut off their water supply. Vikings pillaged. Olaf and Ivar stayed in Strathclyde for the winter and went back to Dublin with treasures and slave they got in Scotland. The forced the King of Scotland, Constantine I to give them public recognition.

8 SIZE OF THE GREAT HEATHEN ARMY

HISTORIANS CAN'T AGREE on a size for this army. Every one of them has a varying estimate for its size. The minimalist scholars like Pete Sawyer, this great army just might have been a lot smaller than originally thought.

In the law code of the King of Wessex, King Ine provided a definition of what army meant which was any invading party or army that contains more than a total of thirty-five men.

Sawyer researched and found a table of Viking ships and noticed that each ship could only carry about 32 men which led to his conclusion that the entire army could not have consisted of any more than about 1,000 men. Some other scholars gave higher estimates. One said that several thousand men were part of the invasions of the Seine. This same scholar stated that the bases to accommodate these armies have not yet been found. Several historians in the 1990's thought that this Great Heathen Army probably had members in the lower thousands, but new research has found that there is still room for some debate.

More than likely, the army developed because of the raids in France. The Emperor had a conflict with his sons. One of these sons brought in the Vikings' support. When the war was over, the Vikings discovered that the towns and monasteries that were situated along the rivers were very vulnerable to attacks. The chance of getting rich drew the Vikings into this area, and it wasn't long before all the rivers on the West coast of France had been raided by the Vikings. In 862, the king of West-France responded to the raids by fortifying all the towns and making sure the rivers were defended. This caused problems for the Vikings to get on land. The lower river and coastal regions were mainly undefended. To stay out of reach of the Vikings, religious groups moved inland. With all these changes in France, the Vikings decided to turn to England.

The majority of the army was made up of both Norwegian and Danish Vikings. A lot of the goods that were unearthed in Repton were mostly of

Norwegian origin. This indicated that a large part of the army more than likely Norwegian. These had been raiding in Britain and around the Irish Sea. The Great Heathen Army was made up of many different groups that grouped together under one leader.

When the Vikings were defeated by King Aethelwulf in 851, they then chose to move north to East Anglia. The army was led by Ragnar's sons: Ivar the Boneless, Ubba, Bjorn Ironside, and Halfdan. The stories say the invasion led by these brothers came about due to the death of their father by King Aella of Northumbria.

In 871, Bagsech brought the Great Summer Army and reinforced the Great Heathen Army and turned their attention back to Wessex.

9 RAGNAR LOTHBROK: REAL MAN OR MYTH?

R AGNAR'S STORY HAS been told through mostly sagas and stories
that are not reliable. These stories are full of myth and legend with
very few facts that can be confirmed by reliable sources. Scandinavia during
this time was illiterate. Very few records are around to support these
fantastical claims. There are two sources from the 1300's that give the best
records about Ragnar. The *Gesta Danorum* as written by the Danish
Historian Saxo Grammaticus and Krakumal which is an Icelandic poem
that romanticizes Ragnar's death. Ragnar's exploits and those of his sons
are recorded in the poem *Hattalykill* of the Orkney Islands. Ragnar is said to
be a descendant of Odin who is the Viking God of War. Ragnar was the
son of Sigurd Ring and Alfild. He received the nickname of Lodbrok or
Lothbrok because of his choice of fashion. He was famous for wearing a
strange coat and trousers made from animal skins. In the written histories
of Ragnar, he is known to have married two brave shieldmaidens, Lagertha
and Queen Aslaug. He fathers his famous sons with these two women.

Historically speaking, the life of Ragnar Lothbork can only be decided
by looking at the places and times that are covered by written facts. The
fact of his true existence doesn't have a firm hold. Many have commented
on *Gesta Danorum*, Saxo's account that Ragnar is a being that can to be made
by marrying differing and confusing events that came to pass while Ragnar
was king. It can be noted that many events give credit to Ragnar being
associated with many legendary figures who have more relevance than
Ragnar himself.

These figures include:

- King Horik I
- King Reginfrid
- A King that ruled a part of Denmark and caused a conflict with Haralk Klak
- Reginherus, who led an attack on Paris in the mid-9th century
- Rognvald of the Irish Annals

The main thing that makes this question a difficult one to answer is that the question itself is ambiguous. So, before we can discuss this, the question needs to be defined more clearly. We are looking at two totally opposite extremes. A skeptic is definitely able to ask whether or not something about a person could be historically accurate and they would get the answer of NO and think they were victorious. On the other hand, a historian could ask if there was ever a Viking that lived by the name of Ragnar. They could say the there was a Viking with the name of Ragnar spelled correctly Reginheri that appeared in the Frankish annals, and therefore would be correct in saying that Ragnar did exist. These two accounts are not acceptable when talking about the subject. We need to look at the subject from a different point of view. For Ragnar Lothbrok to be considered a historical figure, there should be documentation that a person by his name, that performed certain acts, actually lived. This does place the burden of proof where it needs to be.

To answer the question: According to some records, it does not appear that Ragnar Lothbrok is an actual historical figure. There are a few more reasons why listed below:

RAGNAR

There is only one Viking that can be found in historical records, that could possibly have the right name. The Viking that was named Reginheri. Reginheri is a Latin form of Ragnar. According to the Frankish annals, Reginheri died in 845. Reginheri could not have taken part in the events that the legendary Ragnar Lothbrok was said to have done since Reginheri died in France in 845.

There isn't any evidence that Reginheri fathered any of the people that eventually became known as the children of Ragnar Lothbrok. The men that became known as his sons may just have been adopted by Ragnar as this was a common thing to do during this period. If they have been adopted, this might have been because their biological parents were killed or it may have been done to ensure dynastic control just like Emperors in

Roman times adopted the people they wanted to be heirs to their throne.

LOTHBROK

Ari a writer who lived in the 1300's made the first mention of Ragnar and Lothbrok as being one person. This name appears for the first time in Gesta Normannorum Ducum. This is a writing by William of Jumieges from around 1070. He called Lothbrok the father or Bjorn Ironside. It has been verified that there was a Viking named Bjorn. Adam or Bremen who was a writer of the time called Ivar, the son of Lodparchus.

RAGNALL

The *Fragmentary Annals of Ireland* that was edited and translated by Joan N. Radner has an interesting item that might relate to the real Ragnar Lothbrok. It talks about a person named Ragnall whose father was Alpdan, who was king of Norway. The things that he took part in before York fell, are conveyed in such a way that it seems as if Ragnall could be Ragnar.

The best argument for saying that yes Ragnar Lothbrok did exist is to agree that they are, in fact, the one and the same. Even though the names are clearly spelled differently, we can assume that they were confused through either translations or how they were pronounced. R.W. McTurk looked at this very thing by focusing on statements that were shown in the sources. He also wanted to see what assumptions needed to be made to make Ragnar a member of a Danish royal family. The fact that making Ragnar a member of the royal family is needed to prove he was a real historical figure is irrelevant. Let's just say that they are indeed the same person and in fact did exist and someone, somewhere just misspelled the names due to an error within the Scandinavian sources. If we say this is the case, there appear to be about six beliefs that are very necessary and another one that is highly desirable:

1. You would have to believe that Adam of Bremen from the late 11th century was accurate when he said that Lodparchus (Lothbrok) was the father of Ivar.
2. You would have to believe that in *The War of the Gaedhil with the Gaill* which is a twelfth-century source was correct when it stated that Halfdan of Dublin, who died in 877 in Ireland, was the son of Ragnall and that this was the same Ragnall that appeared in the *Fragmentary Annals of Ireland.*
3. You would have to believe the *Anglo-Saxon Chronicle* was right when it stated that an unnamed brother was referred to as Ubbe in a later source of Halfdan, and that Ivar died in England in 878. We must

also believe that there was only ONE person with the name of Ubbe that lived in Scandinavia at this particular time.

4.   You would have to believe that the account of Aethelweard is incorrect when it stated that Halfdan was murdered in England in 878. If this happened, that would mean that Halfdan of Dublin who died in 877 in Ireland could not be the same Halfdan that was the brother to Ivar. You would have to believe here as well that there was only one person with the name of Halfdan in Scandinavian at this particular time.

5.   You would have to believe that both of the Halfdans were the same person, and the brother of Ivar. You would have to believe that this Ivar was the same as Adam of Bremen's Ivar. Also, keep in mind that Aethelweard would have you believe that there were indeed two Ivars in the British Isles at this time. Because we all know that there is no way there could be two different people with the same name in the world at the same time.

6.   You would have to believe that the linguists are wrong when they made Lothbroka a feminine name. When a vowel is added to the end of a word, it can change it into a feminine name. Sort of like Spanish does with the words Chico and Chica. Changing the vowels at the end change the pronoun from masculine to feminine.

7.   If Ari, who was the first author to mention Ragnar Lothbrok, is indeed reliable for this information, then you would have to believe that Halfdan of Dublin was indeed to the same Halfdan of Sigifrid that is mentioned in the Annals of Fulda in the year 873. This is in spite of the severe problems that would cause with the chronological order of Ari's genealogies. And again this is assuming there wasn't more than one person with the same name in the same region at the same time.

Giving all these beliefs, it is very easy to see that Ragnar Lothbrok could have easily been a truly historical figure who lived during the Scandinavian. If you look back at any history, the people were always using the same name for several different people. Different regions spelled the same name several different ways, but it was all the same person.

Whether Ragnar Lothbrok was a real man or just a wonderful myth is for each person to interpret for themselves. He was a fierce warrior that gives Scandinavia and the Vikings a colorful history.

CONCLUSION

Thank for making it through to the end of *Ragnar Lothbrok*. Let's hope it was informative and able to provide you with the information that you were looking for.

I hope you enjoyed learning about Ragnar Lothbrok, his wives, his sons, and all his adventures. Whether you think of him as real or myth, I hope you had as much fun reading it as I did writing it.

Finally, if you found this book useful in any way, a review on Amazon is always appreciated!

ABOUT THE AUTHOR

Dustin Yarc is an ambitious Canadian author who writes passionately about his hobbies and areas of expertise such as personal development, spirituality, speedcubing, video games, gardening, and cryptocurrencies. He self-published his first title at the age of eighteen.

Made in the USA
San Bernardino, CA
25 August 2017